OMG

OBSERVATIONAL MARKETING GREATS STRIKES BACK

GEOFF RAMM

First published 2015 by Creative Juice Publishing

www.geofframm.com

ISBN-13: 978-1518737275

ISBN-10: 1518737277

© Copyright Geoff Ramm

Book Design: Mark Moore, Purely Mint Promotions

Graphic Illustrations: Ian West

Copywriter: Liz Hardy, Plays With Words

Helen Stothard, HLS Publishing Solutions

RAVING REVIEWS

"You can keep your 4-P's of the Marketing Mix – Geoff Ramm has outdone himself this time with real life, gritty examples of brand-new and outstanding marketing ideas that are in the main quick, simple and achievable for businesses of all sizes. Whether you're an aspiring start up entrepreneur or an executive in a multi-national corporation there is incredible inspiration for you all here. Look out mundane marketing, Geoff is striking back!"

Michael Arnot, MD, Unique Speaker Bureau

"OMG Strikes Back is pure genius – I couldn't put it down. It's packed with simple ideas and stories to shake you out of your marketing rut in two minutes or less. Every page had me scribbling down ideas for my clients and my business – before I had even finished the book I had emailed a client with suggestions to make their exhibition stand at a national conference more engaging and memorable. Geoff is the one person on this planet who gets me really excited about marketing. His book will give you permission to have fun, to embrace your quirky, to stand out and to be unforgettable. It will change the way you think about marketing forever. I love love love it!"

Emma Sutton, Queen of Diamonds

"Geoff's ability to mix valuable marketing content, useful tools and humour into his stories and books is what makes him a great author and an excellent speaker. It is also what makes this book an absolute pleasure to read. Geoff's personal stories leave you wondering what kind of creative solution and OMG spin he will come up with for a variety of clients and partners. Geoff also includes cases from a variety of brands and other marketing geniuses which makes this book even more useful and inspirational. This book is an easy but incredibly powerful read for anyone interested in taking their service and marketing to the next level. Reading OMG Strikes Back left me feeling creative and reignited my excitement for marketing."

Christina Hinze Jorgensen, MD, A-Speakers, Denmark

"Our marketing team in Melbourne had the absolute pleasure of spending time with Geoff. He has an incredible eye for spotting moments of innovation and creative genius – and challenged our team to think differently and build raving fans without the need for huge promotional budgets. His new book truly replicates the impact he had on our team, the OMG wall is a tool we have implemented with great success. Geoff has left us wanting more and we can't wait to bring him back to Australia"
Joseph Lyons, Executive General Manager, REA Group, Australia

'Geoff Ramm in his own inimitable style makes us laugh, think and question our own marketing activities. The insights Geoff provides are invaluable and will certainly assist in inspiring, stimulating and motivating all of us to improve our own communications. It is well worth a read. Thanks Geoff'
Grant Leboff, Sticky Marketing Club Limited

"No marketing budget and/or no marketing resource is a familiar tale but what can you do about it? For a start you can read the following pages, take just one of the ideas it will inspire and put it into practice. Geoff manages to describe, in a way any business owner can understand, in ideal bite sized chunks, just how you can make very little go a long way. Finally a business/marketing book that is easy to read, understand and most importantly act upon."
Martin Robertson, Sales Manager, Kilfrost Limited

"Once again the observational guru successfully and entertainingly takes us on a journey through some lateral marketing initiatives as well as gently pointing out how we all at times manage to miss the obvious!
Stewart Pierce, Financial and Commercial Director, Parker Building Supplies Ltd

"OMG Strikes Back continues a long line of exceptionally inspirational yet practical revelations from Mr Ramm. My recommendations to see Geoff or read his books far outstretches any other individual I have encountered, my dog eared copy of Celebrity Service and OMG marketing stand testimony to that. See him speak, read the book have the pleasure of his company as an Advisor, your creativity and thirst for excellence will be reenergised."

Nicki Clark, Chief Operating Officer, BE Group

"Geoff Ramm first inspired me to become a marketer 7 years ago... And he is still doing it today. I was excited for this book but wondering, can it be all it's cracked up to be? Yes it is, and it's better! This book should be on every marketeers shelf; it's refreshing, straight to the point and it tells a great story which is essential for effective marketing".

Esther Damary-Thompson, Media & Marketing Manager, Forward And Thinking

"Rarely does a sequel live up to the original and when Geoff asked me if I would write a few words about his follow up to OMG I was excited and nervous to see if he could do it again.

If you're looking for tips to help you market and grow your business then OMG Strikes Back is the book for you. Easy to read and digest, thought provoking from start to finish and guaranteed to stimulate those creative juices to give you all the ideas you need for your next marketing campaign.

I've already put one of the ideas into practice that resulted in an order the same day.

OMG Strikes Back - and blows the original away!!

Jamie Stewart Managing Director, Bumblebee Digital Ltd

WHEN THE COMPETITION GOES ONE WAY DO YOU FOLLOW THEM OR DO YOU

OG EHT REHTO YAW?

SUTHERLAND COFFEE COMPANY

LONGCHAMP

It's the summer
~~£19.99~~ £12.99

REMEMBERING THE TITANIC

Colmans
Award Winning
Fish & Chips

↑ 🅼 ⓘ 🅿 Free

Arbeia
Roman Fort

•••○○ O2-UK 📶   13:44

News Feed

📝 Status   📷 Photo   📍 Check In

Cotels Serviced Apartments
Shared a photo
Stand 8160, Olympia, London

@TeamCotels going "quackers" #BTShow #GiveaDuck

Caution: This Product
Contains Natural Rubber
Latex Which May cause
Allergic Rea
Latex cond
to preven
HIV/AIDS
Before us
directions.

coming soon...

arousing
the **BUY**
curious

ArousingTheBuyCurious.com

bonjour
SCHOOL PHOTOGRAPHY

PIT
DEP
ARN

CELEBRITY
SERVICE
BY GEOFF RAMM

FOREWORD

First of all, you need to know this is the precise type of book that I love - sharply designed, beautifully laid out, visual, fun, engaging, and smart.

Second of all, you need to know that this author, Geoff Ramm, is the type of speaker, expert, and change agent that your organization, your members, your employees, and your team will love listening to.

Why?

Because Geoff knows that at the intersection of intelligence, humility, humor, surprise, delight, marketing wisdom, and sales savvy lies... well, success. Pure and simple.

As a marketing speaker and marketing author myself, I know there's a ton of rubbish published every minute around the world on the subjects of marketing, sales, and business development. What you're holding in your hand right now is a stand-out gem and a rare gift.

Are you responsible for marketing results? Geoff wrote this book for YOU.

Are you responsible for sales results? Geoff wrote this book for YOU.

Are you an entrepreneur, executive, CEO, business owner, association executive, conference producer, or meeting planner who wants to shake up the status quo, wake your people up to their potential and performance, and make great things happen for YOUR customers and clients? If so, Geoff wrote this book for YOU.

In the pages that follow, you'll laugh, you'll cry, you'll think, and you'll change the way you look at EVERYTHING in your business. And more important, you'll change the way you ACT. Because as you've already experienced, only action creates results.

But then you'll have another problem on your hands - you'll be the only one in your organization who "gets it."

You'll have to fight and claw and argue your way through meetings. You'll have to struggle to escape the commodity thinking that keeps your products and services and people stuck in mediocrity. And you'll be constantly frustrated by your colleagues' inaction, backwards thinking, and fear of breaking through to true category distinction and market domination.

I have an easy solution for you. Do this right now: Buy copies of this book for everyone you work with. You'll thank me later.

Truly.

And now, sit back, get comfortable, and get ready to skyrocket your success with the brilliant ideas, principles, practices, and tools of OMG2.

YOU are #1 for takeoff. Fasten your seatbelts and away we goooooooooo....

David Newman,
Author of Do It! Marketing: 77 Instant-Action Ideas to Boost Sales, Maximize Profits, and Crush Your Competition

CONTENTS

"WHEN CREATIVITY MEETS OPPORTUNITY

GREAT MARKETING HAPPENS"

Dedicated to Hayley, Grace & Elliot x

WHO IS GEOFF?

Born in South Shields, England, two days after Christmas Day, Geoff still has the ambition to become the next Milk Tray Man - the TV commercial that captured his imagination when he was just six years old.

Geoff's favourite subject at Whitburn Comprehensive School was business studies, and he went on to study marketing at South Tyneside College, before graduating from University of Sunderland Business School.

His first marketing role – at an Enterprise Agency - involved helping hundreds of entrepreneurs to launch and develop their own businesses; he then moved on to work alongside some of the world's most iconic motoring brands.

On Saturday 1st March 2002, Geoff started up his own business, Mercury Marketing, and in 2008 launched his speaking brand Geofframm.com. He's since written two books – OMG Observational Marketing Greats, and Celebrity Service.

He's created marketing ideas that have become legend, and has inspired audiences around the world with his energetic, humorous, creative take on the world of marketing and customer service. He's a multi-award-winning speaker, who has shared the stage with some of the most recognised business leaders and personalities in the world.

Geoff is a Fellow of the PSA (Professional Speaking Association) in the United Kingdom, and is one of a handful of speakers to be awarded the PSAE – the Professional Speaking Award of Excellence, in recognition of his speaking excellence and professionalism.

He lives in Boldon, South Tyneside, is Husband to Hayley, and Dad to Grace and Elliot.

He loves pizza, cider and supports Sunderland AFC, but don't hold the last one against him.

ALSO

AVAILABLE
ONLINE

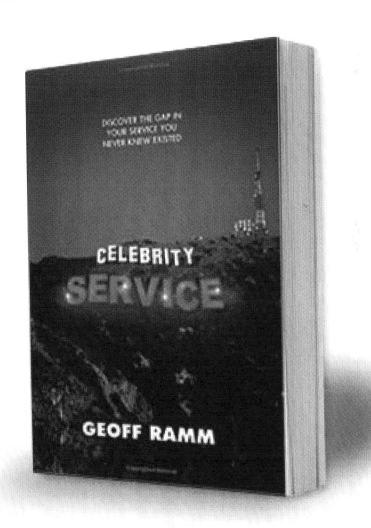

INTRODUCING STRIKES BACK

In a marketing galaxy not so far far away, the second instalment of some of the most eye opening and jaw dropping moments has landed, with the arrival of OMG Strikes Back.

Welcome aboard.

Jam-packed within these pages are the real life examples, ideas and observations, that are sure to inspire you to create your very own OMG Moments; the moments that will enable you to stop your customers in their tracks.

Although affectionately called Strikes Back, sadly, this book does not feature marketing ideas from Hoth, Dagobah or Cloud City, however, it does promise to take you to far far away places, without the need to jump into hyper-space, have vaccinations, or suffer any unnecessary jet lag.

From Manchester to Melbourne, Tallinn to Tyneside, and Johannesburg to Jarrow, see how brands of all sizes and sectors have dared to engage, attract, and take all steps necessary to stand out from their competition.

Strikes Back also has some extended scenes including: Carpe Diem, Up Close And..., as well as Stand And Deliver. And, for the very first time, I am revealing the two techniques that I use, time and time again, to create ideas for myself and my clients; techniques guaranteed to help you and your team to unearth great OMG moments! Fear not, it will only take a couple of minutes of your time, but be prepared to make some changes to your office wall in the process!

Warning: this is not a strategy book, and it's not a planning book either - it's just full of the people, businesses and brands who have stopped me in my tracks and who have a passion for going the other way.

The image on the cover is a clue as to how to use this book: treat it like a little book of matches; take one of these ideas, adapt it to your business, strike it, stand back, let it take hold... and see what happens, and what new creativity it ignites.

Marketing, of course, has changed, and as the world sways heavily to online and digital media we can't necessarily do what we've always done before. However, our basic human instincts have stayed the same, so however you execute your future ideas, please remember to give the customer what they want, and to add extra traction by making them laugh, entertaining them, surprising them, and making them feel special; you can even go as far as exciting or thrilling them, too.

I hope you enjoy my third book – the second in the OMG series – and please, please, please, email me (geoff@geofframm.com) and tell me the ideas you come up with and the successes they bring you, as there's a good chance I'll be talking about your business sometime soon.

Wishing you every future success.

I'VE ONLY GOT £10

My very first job in marketing was at the CDC Enterprise Agency. A wonderful organisation dedicated to advising and supporting start-up and existing SME's (Small Medium Enterprises) in Durham City and Chester Le Street in the North East of England. My role there was as a marketing advisor and I loved every single minute. Every client, every day, was a different experience that would test your marketing knowledge and creativity. There was the dog groomer, the puppet lady, the furniture maker, the restaurant, a counselling website, a carpet cleaner, a milkshake bar and of course a list wouldn't be complete without a teddy bear shop. Despite every entrepreneur being different they all had the same burning question...

How can I get more customers?

My first month involved shadowing my manager Sue Parkinson. Listening, observing and watching what clients wanted and needed was fascinating and a seismic shift away from studying business at University.

One month on and I was about to be let loose in advising entrepreneurs, start ups and small businesses. I was the only marketing person at CDC so as you can imagine my diary filled up with ease on the hour, every hour and weeks in advance.

With a good degree firmly behind me I couldn't wait to get started in my career, but I'll never forget my very first client.

Monday morning 8:45am I awaited my first appointment, and I was ready; ready with a wealth of marketing knowledge to share. Market segmentation, strategic planning, positioning strategies were all of the things I'd learnt from business school, so every business needed them, right?

8:55am the buzzer sounded downstairs to signal that my first client had arrived. I was nervous, and from nowhere my palms began to mirror Niagra falls.

In walked Gary Thompson from Pelton Window Cleaners. We shook hands and he sat down..... "How can I help?" The first question any advisor would ask.

Gary looked me in the eye and bluntly said "I need more customers". He then reached into his trouser pocket and pulled out a £10 note and as he placed it on the desk he said "And that's all I've got to do it".

To say I was shocked was an understatement. Where do I go from here? And where do I fit in the part about positioning, planning and segmentation? In that moment I mentally threw 95% of my degree out the window and proceeded to concentrate on his need for more customers.

I asked so many questions in the first 50 mins of our meeting and we only had 10 minutes to go.... I was struggling to come up with any ideas to get him noticed and to attract customers for his miniscule budget.

Please remember this was a time before YouTube, Twitter, LinkedIn, and Facebook... It was a time when you had limited options, radio, tv, flyers, direct mail, yellow pages and adverts in the local press, that was it!

My final question that morning held the answer.... "Tell me Gary, is there anything different, weird or even wonderful that you do?"

He pondered for a moment and said "Yes". "We've just been on a course and me and the lads have received our abseiling certificate".

"That's great Gary, but what about the business?"

"It is for the business. We can now abseil down buildings to clean windows. This means we don't have to charge for scaffolding or for the cherry picker machines, so essentially this saves the client a lot of money."

A week later I was stood on top of the Louisa Leisure Centre in Stanley, County Durham (possibly the windiest place on earth) taking photographs as Gary and his team lept off the edge. Not one for heights I stretched my arm over the side, holding my camera and clicked to my hearts content. I took the film to be developed and two days later chose the best images to post to the local media with the very first news release I had ever written. (I told you this was some time ago).

One week later I successfully managed to achieve a full page 3 spread in the Evening Chronicle newspaper. If he had of paid for this space as an advert it would have cost thousands.....

The hundreds of clients that came through my office throughout the 3 and a half years I was there taught me one valuable lesson, which has been part of my marketing DNA ever since. Start with a £10 note and see what can be achieved. When your back is pressed against the wall and you have limited room for manoeuvre - THAT is when you become creative.

In that time I had achieved over half a million pounds worth of PR through radio, press and television and it is something I am extremely proud of. So much so that when I left the enterprise agency I took my original copies with me (I always bought two) and I still have them to this day (including 2 VHS video cassettes).

My very first client, my very first PR success and all for under £10. (slight confession - I was not the greatest photographer so they sent a professional out afterwards).

With a heavy heart I left the enterprise agency but it was the right time to move on, it was time to test myself again and boy was I tested....

He knows the ropes

High hopes as window cleaner ditches his ladders

By CHARLES WESTBERG

GARY Thompson is the window cleaner with altitude.

His polished service is condemning ladders, buckets and chamois leathers as things of the past.

The man with a head for heights is mopping up customers all over Britain – 15 years after starting his first round.

The 37-year-old is one of an elite band of abseiling cleaners who can tackle any building anywhere at any time.

He said: "We can jump off a building 800ft tall to clean the windows or need be – or ascend them going up by rope.

"It's a lot safer than using cradles, there have been that many accidents with them, some of them fatal.

"They are also expensive to maintain costing thousands of pounds to be serviced."

Gary, who runs Felton Window Cleaners, near Stanley, Co Durham, got hooked on abseiling after attending a specialist course – the Bristol Window Cleaning Academy.

His amazing tricks of the trade mean no job is too big.

"Any building can be accessed," he said. "If we can get onto a pitched roof or the top floor of a building we can

NO JOB TOO DIFFICULT – Gary Thompson, pictured below, will clean windows no matter how difficult they are to reach

anchor our ropes and let ourselves down.

"We won't be beaten we will do it vertically, horizontally, even going down head first if necessary."

Gary and his five staff still

do basic window cleaning but the abseiling is taking off. Current contracts range from Hartlepool Power Station to the Hermitage Comprehensive School in Chester-le-Street. They also do work in factories from cleaning interiors or beams to changing bulbs in inaccessible lights.

Their services are in great demand in the south. Work is already lined up in Bristol and Cambridge over the Christmas period and they hope to land a contract to clean stately homes in Ireland.

"In 10 years time you won't see a window cleaner with a ladder," Gary added.

NO JOB TOO HIGH – Gary puts his abseiling skills to good use as he conquers the highest and most inaccessible buildings to clean windows

MISTLETOE
AND MOTORS

My next role was as a Marketing Manager for a motor retail group in the North East of England.

It was a world away from working with entrepreneurs and start ups as there were 6 global brands to support, promote and market: Honda, Toyota, Chrysler, Fiat, Suzuki and Citroen; each one with differing demographics, demanding different marketing approaches.

The budgets in motor marketing were rather different, too. There were no more £10's put on the table; now we were talking TV campaigns, annual newspaper advertising strategies, and radio promotions to help market special events and launch new models.

The role was huge, exciting, and challenging, and I loved it.

However, I also went there with the mentality I had gained from my time at the CDC Enterprise Agency - what could we do if we only had £10?

I was fortunate to be at the company for the biggest change in recent UK motoring history – the brand new number plate which would take us from one registration date per year, to two. For the first time, the numbers in the centre of the plate would reveal the date in which the cars were registered, and the letters would signify where in the UK the car was registered. The very first plate would feature the numbers 51, and would be unveiled to the public on the 1st September.

It was boom time for the industry, as it seemed almost every motorist wanted the new style plate, so there were floods of customers coming to part-exchange their older cars. The downside to this was that every dealership had a larger than healthy stockpile of used cars on their hands, which simply couldn't be moved. Well, not without some marketing intervention or perhaps an OMG moment or two…

I remember sitting in a board meeting with the Managing Director, Operational Director, Marketing Director, many of the Dealer Principles, and the advertising agency. The schedule of marketing activities was handed out to everyone for the next quarter... October was the usual busy schedule, November a little less, but December was blank!
There must be some mistake!

So I had to ask the question, "What's happened to December?"

"What do you mean?" said the Managing Director

"Well there is no activity in December, why not?"

"Well Geoff, you see, you don't sell cars in December."

"Why?" (I pretty much knew the answer, but I still had to ask).

"Well, December is a short month. Everyone is in holiday party mode; people are buying presents not cars, and it's an expensive time of the year."

"So what have we done over previous years to sell cars?"

"Nothing. You don't sell cars, so we don't market to sell cars."

"So in other words a double negative and we will always be right?"

The room fell silent and the MD said: "I am guessing you have an idea?"

"Yes, I do."

The idea was a simple two-pronged approach.

1. Use the power of our customer database.

2. Don't rely on customers coming to us - let's take the cars out to the general public.

After a Wild West style, middle-of-the-street standoff complete with tumbleweed......... the board granted me permission to execute my ideas.

Idea 1:

We embarked on one of our biggest ever direct mailer campaigns. I rang around and obtained the best car deal from every dealership and we created a large colourful mailer. It was placed in a clear plastic bag so the outside looked like Christmas gift wrapping, all ready to open. But where was the OMG twist? I also needed a way to gauge my campaign's success, whilst intriguing the customer enough to open, read and react, so I came up with the idea of including a sprig of mistletoe inside every one of the 26,000 mailer!

You could feel there was something inside and when you opened to find out what was there, the message read 'Kiss goodbye to your car this Christmas'. And 'If you bring the mistletoe into the dealership you'll be entered into a draw for a video camera.'

Idea 2:

The Metro Centre is one of Europe's largest indoor shopping centres so you can imagine the queues and hordes of last minute shoppers in the week leading up to Christmas. I took a calculated risk and placed two Honda cars outside the entrance of the Marks & Spencer store, under cover and away from the winter elements.

Seeing the creation of these ideas unfold, the MD kindly offered to support them further, with a TV commercial and press campaign. I said I didn't need it, but they were adamant so the two other activities went ahead with the same 'Kiss goodbye to your old car this Christmas' theme.

In the last week of November I personally called around each dealership and handed out my own questionnaire for every Salesperson to ask everyone who walked into their dealership during December - Q. What made you come in today - mailer? MetroCentre? TV? Newspapers? On January 4th I collected all of the data from the sales teams.

The results were as follows - more people came from the mailer than the TV commercial and every newspaper combined!
Oh, and two Honda Accords worth £40k+ were purchased on Christmas Eve morning, by customers who had seen the vehicles and chatted to the team at the Metro Centre.

It was a huge team effort, as myself and the Marketing team sat on the floor for days on end stapling 26,000 sprigs of mistletoe into the brochure (I don't think they've ever forgiven me!)

The Result:
In short, we sold cars in December. The dealerships were unusually busy, and a few of the younger salesmen were chased around by a couple of customers with mistletoe in their hands.

Rules I have lived by ever since:
Never trust a double negative - you'll always be right.
Don't accept what's gone before is the best or only way forwards.
Your database is the backbone of your marketing - Your database is the backbone of your marketing - thought I'd put it in twice so you don't forget.

And the OMG moment was just a small piece of plastic that caused customers to be intrigued to react.

And one final idea... I couldn't just let the biggest number plate change go without giving it a real creative spin, so to celebrate 51, I came up with an Area 51 style campaign: radio commercials were in the style of X Files, dealerships were decked out in an alien theme etc. 14 years on and I've yet to see any motor dealership use the numbers to their creative advantage. Such a wasted, wasted opportunity.

SOME TIMES

Coming up with, and indeed executing an OMG Moment or two is not the easiest thing to achieve. Sometimes you have to observe your marketing activities from a distance, question them, and wonder if they can be improved upon.

Before we strike the first of those OMG marketing book matches, let's take a light-hearted look at some not-quite-so OMG moments...

Offers & Promotions:

If you are not experiencing a great return on your offers and promotions, don't worry, just make them a little more appealing than this one....

Be Honest:

Is it not time for marketers and businesses to come out and literally tell the truth? Wouldn't that be refreshing? Like a business I spotted in Keswick in the Lake District...

Testimonials:

Written testimonials are great; video testimonials are even better, but what about a visual testimoanial? - make sure you choose a happy customer!

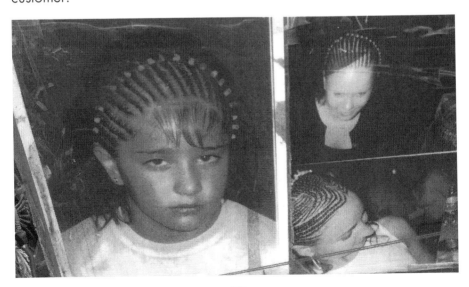

Christmas:

Sometimes you need to avoid the obvious...

FESTIVE MENU
Available from 25th November 2014 to
1st January 2015
(excluding 25th, 26th and 31st December)

CHRISTMAS DAY MENU
Available 25th December 2014 only

BOXING DAY MENU
Available on 26th December 2014 only

NEW YEAR'S EVE FEAST MENU
Available on 31st December 2014 only

Children's Festive Menus
are also available

It's beginning to look a lot like Christmas

Multi Channels:

Remember, not all of your messages will translate across all communication channels! This was an interesting sticker to place on a book...

CARPE DIEM

Seize the day and you'll seize the moment for your business.

There are monumental moments happening all around the world right now, but the question remains, are you ready for them? Do you know they are coming? And if you don't, can you predict and then act quickly enough to grab a slice of the traction?

The moments I am referring to could be political, environmental, legal, sporting, entertainment, or music-based, and they will centre around the biggest, head-line-grabbing story to come out of that event. For example: a Royal birth, a footballer biting an opponent at the World Cup, or the release of a raunchy movie.

This next section will help you to see these emerging stories and global moments as opportunities, and will shift your thinking away from 'That has nothing to do with me' to 'Can we do something on the back of this?' In other words, when Madonna fell from the stage at the Brit Awards, did you watch it in your living room and think 'OMG that's awful' or did you think 'OMG that's awful, but I have an idea!'?

Lights Out

Probably the greatest example of reacting to a global event was set by Oreo cookies during Super Bowl XLVII when a sudden loss of power during the third quarter turned all the lights out! Within those darkest of 34 minutes, the social media and design teams at Oreo quickly set to work to create an image and tweet that would set the social networking universe alight: "Power Out? No Problem" with an image of an Oreo cookie sat in a dimly lit corner, and the caption: "You can still dunk in the dark".

The tweet itself caused 15,000 immediate retweets and over 20,000 likes on Facebook.

But how did they produce something so creative and so quickly? Oreo had a 15-person team ready to respond to any event or stand-out Super Bowl moment that they thought would make great engagement. Ironically, when the lights went out, the lightbulb moment came on.

Anyone reading this story may not have a 15-strong creative team watching the game and praying something significant will happen, but that's not the important message here. The point is: Oreo knew! Oreo knew the Super Bowl was coming up, knew the coverage and attention it would get on social networks, and they were prepared. They had copywriters, designers and strategists waiting to take advantage of anything that happened; waiting for their Carpe Diem OMG moment. As a result of their creativity and quick response, they were the talk of the Super Bowl that year, above any of the paid-for advertised brands, because they were prepared.

Boy Oh Boy

One of the biggest news stories to hit the UK, and, indeed the world, was the birth of the future King of England, Prince George.

Camera crews and reporters from all over the world were camped outside of the hospital entrance for weeks on end, ready to snap William and Kate entering the hospital, and that very first glimpse of the new baby Prince when the family emerged onto the hospital steps.

Within seconds of the news breaking, social and traditional media were in a state of 'Royal Birth' frenzy, and mere moments after the news broke I spotted the first OMG tweet. It was from Delta Airlines... it featured a baby playing with a mobile above him, but instead of the usual teddy bears and cute animals, the mobile featured miniature Delta aircraft. The tweet read: "It's a boy! Welcome, Prince of Cambridge. We can't wait to show you the world. #RoyalBaby" Now, the chances of Prince George getting on a Delta airline flight may be slim, but the image soon went viral.

The second tweet I saw was another fine creative example from Oreo cookies; the image was of a red velvet cushion with gold trim and tassels, displaying a bottle of babies' milk and an Oreo cookie leaning against it. The caption said: "Prepare the Royal milk". It went viral.

Next up were the kings and queens of personalisation, Starbucks. They sent out an image of a large, medium and small cup. The large cup had a golden crown on it with the hand written name William on it. The medium cup had a silver crown with the name Kate written on it and the baby cup had a tiny crown on top but there was no hand written name (he hadn't been named at this stage). It went viral.

So I am sitting in the lounge with my Mac on my knee, replying to emails, and in the corner of the room the television was showing the coverage of the birth. I noticed the news reader kept going back to Buckingham Palace, and then back to the news room, and then back to the Palace. This went on for at least 20 minutes, so I wondered what all the fuss was about, and what was the importance of the Palace? I turned the volume up and found out they were awaiting the official announcement which would be put in a frame and then placed on a golden easel for the world to see.

Here was my opportunity.

I quickly screen-grabbed the television image and placed the cover of my first book onto the easel. The caption said "OMG arriving soon, author and content doing fine". 24 hours later I had 42 additional sales of the book, which I attribute to this post on Twitter and Facebook.

So how did you use this story to gain momentum for your business? C'mon, you had 9 months to think of something!!!

Thankfully another entrepreneur did just that…

Katie & Kate

My good friend, fitness coach extraordinaire, fellow speaker, and star of the BBC One television show, The Apprentice, Katie Bulmer-Cooke, created her 'Fit Mummy Manual' to help new mums get back in shape after their birth, but what she told me she needed was a game changer… This is what she did.

"It was New Year 2013. I wanted to get the Fit Mummy Manual brand out there, but I didn't have a big marketing budget (or even a small one come to that!). Even if I could have afforded it, I didn't want to put it in the hands of a marketing and PR agency. I wanted to do it myself, but I'm not (wasn't) a marketer, and I'm not an expert in PR.

"I was sitting at my desk one day, wondering how I could get some good publicity without spending any money. I can't remember what triggered it, but suddenly I had an idea - Royal Endorsement!

"The hottest news at the time was the impending arrival of Prince George, the royal baby, son and heir to Prince William and Kate Middleton, the Duchess of Cambridge. I Googled Clarence House, copied down the address, grabbed a Fit Mummy DVD and a jiffy bag, packaged it up with a covering letter. I took it down to the post office, thinking, "I've got nothing to lose, and fortune favours the brave!"

"What was the worst that could happen? The DVD and packaging cost less than a pound! So I sent it off, not knowing whether anything would come of it. To my complete surprise a couple of weeks later I received a letter back from St James' Palace, written on beautiful parchment with the royal seal on the envelope and an embossed logo at the top, from Rebecca, Kate Middleton's assistant, thanking me for sending the Fit Mummy Manual DVD. I couldn't believe it.

"But then I started to wonder what I could do with it?

"My first action was to call the local paper, The Sunderland Echo, and the local radio station, and managed to get myself on the air, telling them that Kate had a copy of my DVD and that I had the letter to prove it. The next thing I knew, the national press had picked it up and I was being asked to do a whole bunch of interviews. Then I found out that on the other side of the world, the Australian and New Zealand press had covered the story, and it was all over their women's magazines too! Of course, out in the Commonwealth, anything to do with the royal baby was huge news! The story made it into women's magazines all around the world. I had my game-changer!

"I'm not a great believer in outsourcing, especially when I can learn how to do things for myself. With the Princess and the PR, if I had outsourced my marketing, who's to say that my agency would ever have had that idea, and that they'd have been able to turn it around so quickly? For sure it would have cost a lot more than the one single pound I'd invested in the whole thing!

"Now don't get me wrong, the letter wasn't one of great detail - I won't make it out to be something it wasn't. But I grabbed the opportunity with both hands, and yes, milked it a little! But it gave me a great chance to help educate thousands of women on pre and post-natal fitness.

"On the back of the royal 'connection', America started to become interested in what we were doing, and we now have more customers in the USA than our home market. We also picked up customers in Australia, New Zealand, Japan, Mexico, France and Canada."

ST JAMES'S PALACE

From: Miss Rebecca Deacon
        Private Secretary to HRH The Duchess of Cambridge

Private and Confidential

18th January, 2013

Dear Katie and Kelly (if I may).

The Duchess of Cambridge has asked me to write and thank you for your letter of 12th December, in which you make Her Royal Highness aware of the services you provide as pre and post natal exercise specialists.

It was extremely kind of you to take the trouble to write as you did, and The Duchess would have me send you her warmest thanks and best wishes.

Yours sincerely,

Rebecca Deacon

Ms. Katie Bulmer-Cooke and Ms. Kelly Rennie,
The Fit Mummy Manual

50 Shades Of Promotion

Ah, yes, yes, yes, yes.........! the biggest selling book of recent years: 50 Shades of Grey. There has been so much hype, talk, and publicity around the book, and then later the movie, but I don't want to concentrate on that just now; I want to tell you about two brands that saw the opportunity to build traction off the back of this much-talked-about release.

Firstly, the book. The UK supermarket chain Sainsbury's stocked the book on one of its shelves, but interestingly enough they placed it beside another product – perhaps they saw an opportunity to cross-sell? A photograph was taken (it could have been from a customer), posted online, and it went viral. Beside the books were packs of... wait for it... batteries!

A few years on and the movie hit the big screens, with all the associated hype and build-up. During the build-up to premieres and full release, DIY chain B&Q sent out a memo to all its staff, which was leaked to the web. The memo asked everyone to be aware that after the movie was released they may be asked for certain products as used/seen in the film, for example: tape, cable ties, rope, etc.

What happened next was a sprinkling of OMG gold dust as television, radio, newspapers and social media all featured, covered, and commented on the leaked memo. From the Guardian newspaper to the MTV music channel, B&Q grabbed this opportunity and attracted global publicity. Of course, the memo was a smokescreen, a fake, it wasn't really sent out to staff, but it was a wonderful stunt that seized the day and gained the DIY chain a huge amount of exposure.

Brucie Bonus

2014, FA Cup Final, Wembley, London, Arsenal versus Hull City.
I was in the departure lounge at Cardiff International Airport when I looked up at the TV screen and watched the 'and finally' story on Sky Sports. It was all about a company commemorating Hull City reaching the FA Cup Final... with a toilet seat???
Step forwards Jenny Smith, Media Relations Manager at Ideal Standard, a toilet manufacturer based in Hull. They came up with the idea of a

commemorative orange and black striped (the team's colours) toilet seat and when you lifted the lid there was an image of the Hull City manager, Steve Bruce.

This was such an OMG moment that I called Jenny up to congratulate her and to find out more. She told me it was one of those ideas that was so 'tongue in cheek' that they knew it wouldn't get passed by the board for approval – but it did!

21 pieces of coverage were achieved worth around £178,000. Approximately 800 tweets were recorded, with key re-tweeters including Paddy Power bookmakers with 320,000 followers, and Jacqui Oatley, a BBC football commentator with 82,000 followers.

I take my hat off to Jenny for the idea, and to the board for letting creativity quite literally go with the flow.

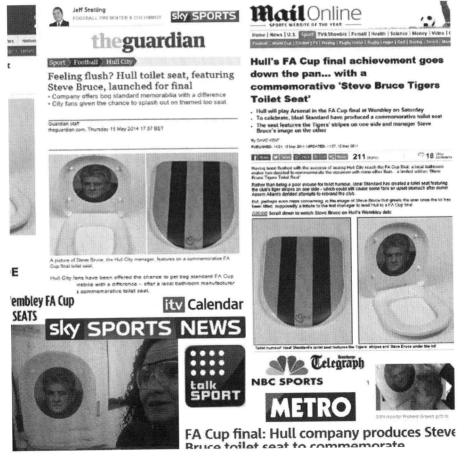

Michael Jackson Plays Wembley 2015

How is this possible? Has the prince of pop been resurrected? Not quite, but Michael Jackson did appear one last time at the home of football.

A year on from the toilet seat story, the FA Cup was about to have another wave of OMG attention.

For those of you that have witnessed the FA Cup draw, it is quite an occasion in England. Teams in the competition are given a number and then numbered balls are drawn randomly out of a bag, one at a time, to determine which teams play each other. The draw for the fifth round started... Preston North End will play... Manchester Utd. A big Lancashire derby, pitting lower league Preston against the global might of the Red Devils.

Up steps Michael Jackson, (no, not that one, but The Other Michael Jackson), a wonderful speaker, who I've had the pleasure of working with many times, and, more importantly, one of my very best friends. Despite living in Johannesburg, Michael was born in Preston and has supported the Lily Whites, as well as the Red Devils, all his life. Can you imagine how eager he was to obtain a ticket? Can you imagine the lengths he would go to for this once-in-a-lifetime match?

The following morning Michael posted this picture on Facebook.

He offered to 'sell a kidney', 'ride a giraffe', or 'swim from Cape Town' for a ticket to the big game! Myself, friends, family, associates, and clients all started to share the image, but what happened next was the opposite of BAD!

The image turned into a story that was quickly picked up by The Sun, BBC Football, Sky News, Talk Sport, and many other localised north west newspapers and radio stations. It was amazing for me to see it all unfold, as Michael and I were texting with updates on which studio or reporter he was going to speak to next. As someone who used to work with Sir Richard Branson, Michael has an uncanny knack for self-promotion, and whenever he was on air he was able to drop in the fact that he was a speaker and what he spoke on (at least twice!) OMG indeed.

The result? Michael and his wife Carol were invited to Wembley by the Football Association, were picked up from Heathrow, and chauffeur driven to the stadium where – inside the actual FA Cup trophy – there were two complimentary tickets to the game. One idea, one photograph, one happy Preston North End fan with a cup full of publicity.

Rainbow Nation

In 2015 the Supreme Court in America brought marriage equality to all 50 states, ruling that same-sex marriage-bans violate the 14th Amendment. This was a landmark moment, celebrated by people across the country, and the rest of the world.

One particularly popular way for people to celebrate and show their support was the addition of a rainbow-stripes filter to Facebook profile pictures, filling timelines with colourful celebrations.

And it wasn't just the general public who were celebrating this momentous ruling; many key brands spotted the opportunity to share the love and increase their reach. Here are some of the most creative that went viral that day…

Levi's simply changed their logo to the rainbow colours.

Tide detergent featured socks in rainbow colours, formed into the shape of a love-heart.

American Airlines tweeted a picture of all their on-board screens filled with the rainbow.

And finally, Kellogg's used a bowl of cereal as the 'O' in 'LOVE', on top of a rainbow place-mat, with the caption: "Love. The Same At Every Table".

My final question on your Carpe Diem moments is a simple one... How prepared are you for future opportunities? You may not have the luxury of 15 people staying up half the night waiting for something to happen, but you can easily create a marketing calendar of events, announcements, arrivals and occasions.

Let me help you get started...

Brit Awards, Grammy's, Oscars, Soccer World Cup, Woman's World Cup, Commonwealth Games, Olympics, Super Bowl, BAFTAS, General Elections, Presidential Elections, Weddings, Births, FA Cup, Wimbledon, US Open, New York Marathon, Film Premieres, Celebrity Marriages, and so on...

WARNING: Do NOT try to promote your brand when negative or controversial news erupts, as it could quite easily backfire on your best intentions. I do question whether all publicity is good publicity!

RISQUE RUDE AND REMEBERED

It's not for every business, and if you are unsure then stay away from this section, but for those of you who wish to be cheeky, mischievous, or simply have some fun with your brand, and your customers then can you push the boundaries to be risqué or even rude?

Here are a selection that made the final cut...

The Granary Restaurant Leith:

Meat a great market stall!

Time for bed in Cape Town?

This is one way to beat Google in Malta!

*"Do you want to eat well? F*** Googel ask us"*

Fancy a mothercuppa in Johannesburg?

Around the corner from West Ham Utd's Bolelyn Ground...

Hanging on to quirky text...

How else could you promote fruit smoothies (melons)?

ETERNAL FLAME

They said the Summer of 2012 would inspire a generation, and they were right.

The Olympic and Paralympic Games held in London were a spectacle like no other, with an abundance of inspiration, fun, and tongue-in-cheek, Monty Pythonesque humour, that only the British could serve up.

But what were your highlights and memories of those few short weeks? The Queen skydiving out of the helicopter with James Bond? A triple gold for the fastest man on earth, Usain Bolt? Mr Bean playing keyboard, the Mobot, or Jess Ennis fulfilling her top-of-the-podium destiny?   There were so many highlights, but who were the businesses and brands who captured the attention throughout the games?

Here are a few that caught my eye…

Minimum Size Maximum Impact

The Javelin thrower takes a swift run up, pulls their arm back as far as they can, and launches what could be a medal-winning, record-breaking throw…

In previous years, a steward would mark the distance and then lift the javelin from the soil, before bringing it back to the white line, but this was all to change in 2012. Mini BMW were the transport/vehicle partners for the 2012 games, and came up with a brilliant way to get their brand into shot. Remote controlled Mini cars raced across the grass after the distance had been marked, then carried the javelin back to the starting point. A lot of social media traction and blogs were written about this and it was great to see live in action.

At the recent Anniversary Games at the Olympic Park, supermarket giants, Sainsburys, used the same technique, but replaced the cars with their home delivery service vans.

Being the main sponsor at any event will give you license to be seen, but you still have to make an impact to ensure you are noticed and talked about long after the event has closed. But what if you are not a main sponsor? How can you direct the attention towards yourself?

On Yer Bike

Innocent were selling their chilled smoothie drinks in bicycle carts – nothing out of the ordinary here, until they gave each bicycle a name – a quirky 'bike' related pun.
Here, I came across Bike Miligan (a take on the famous English comedian, Spike Miligan).
There was also Jimmy Saddle, a spoof of Jimmy Saville – although not too sure how the Innocent brand would stack up beside his name anymore!

Torch Tour

In the weeks leading up to the lighting of the cauldron in the Olympic Stadium, the torch travelled around the UK, passed hand-to-hand by selected runners who made a difference in their local communities. Following the runners, in convoy, were the three main sponsors: Coca Cola, Samsung and Lloyds Bank. Each one of these had a branded bus with a team on-board.

Standing in the pouring rain, Grace, Hayley, and myself, waited all morning to catch a glimpse of the flame as it sped through the coastal village of Whitburn. We could see in the distance the flashing lights from the police motorbikes' escort. Immediately after the runner, the 3 sponsors came slowly past, each of the brand teams jumping off their truck to give onlookers a gift. Lloyds gave out paper hats with their brand on it (shame they weren't giving away money!); Coca Cola were giving away miniature bottles of Coke Zero (but the label was a limited edition 2012 version), and Samsung went for the technological, personalised approach – they displayed the name of every village, town or city they passed through.

Royal Approval

To celebrate the achievements of every gold medal winner from both Olympic and Paralympic Games, The Royal Mail dedicated one of its legendary red post office boxes to each winning athlete, painting it gold in their hometown!

Here is the post box for gold medal swimming sensation Josef Craig, in his hometown of Jarrow, South Tyneside.

FLYING LESSONS

Whether travelling for work or pleasure, flying to destinations around the world has become the norm for many of us, but have you ever really observed the marketing masterpieces that can be found in the air? Here are a selection of flight-related observations to get your creativity soaring...

Double Dutch

The pilot announces to passengers that we are approaching Schiphol airport, and thanks everyone for choosing to fly with KLM. He said he appreciated that we could have chosen any number of carriers. Nice touch.

He then continues, "If you have any comments or suggestions, you can either speak to the cabin crew, visit our website, or go to @klm on Twitter, and we promise to get back to you within the hour." Now there was a challenge which I readily accepted.

A week later, I was making my way back to Schiphol from Quito, Ecuador, so I decided to test their promise, sending the following tweet to see if they would take the bait within 60 minutes...

 @GeoffRamm
Geoff Ramm

Loved speaking for EKOS #ekoscumbree2014 in Ecuador. Great service here at @Marriott Quito. Now ready to go home via @KLM adios x

They replied.

Royal Dutch Airlines ✓
@KLM

@GeoffRamm Are you ready to come back home with us, Geoff? Hope everything went great during your speech for Ekos :-)

14/11/2014 19:17

So I replied back.

@GeoffRamm
Geoff Ramm

Show Conversation

@KLM I certainly am!!! Flying 5:30pm today Quito to Ams - speech went really well thanks!

Sent 4d ago
From Twitter Web Client

Eleven hours later we landed, so I sent out another tweet

Geoff Ramm
@GeoffRamm

Almost home... 3 things why @KLM is best carrier in the skies... 1. Great attentive service 2. Ent choice 3. Gift at the end!

15/11/2014 14:46

And they responded again.

 Royal Dutch Airlines
@KLM

@GeoffRamm Hello Geoff. Thank you for your kind words! We appreciate it :)

15/11/2014 15:05

So I responded.

 @GeoffRamm
Geoff Ramm

 Show Conversation

@KLM and reason number 4 is you reply to tweets within the hour!!! #celebrityservice at its best - cheers!

Sent 3d ago
From Twitter for iPhone

And they responded.

 Royal Dutch Airlines
@KLM

@GeoffRamm You make us blush now, Geoff :-) Thank you, we certainly try to do our best! We like to chat with our people :-)

(We get married later this year!!!)

This was marvellous continuation of communication across two continents, which I hadn't expected, and it was all personalised to me. It was a great experience, and a benchmark was set by KLM which other carriers need to follow and live up to.

So what was the gift I hear you say, which I happily tweeted about? At the time I was travelling, KLM were celebrating their 95th year in business. To mark the occasion, mid-flight the crew would come round the cabin with a selection of miniature houses, filled with Bols liqueur. There were 95 houses in total, and each one was a tiny replica of a building you would find in Amsterdam.

Sadly, I need another 91 houses to complete the set, but you can see the full display in the KLM lounge area. As for my four mini buildings, well, they sit on my memorabilia shelf, but more importantly they serve as a great reminder of their brand. As an additional marketing tactic, the neat idea of creating a collectible series didn't pass me by, either.

How quickly are you responding on social media?
Do you make your response time a promise?
Do you make sure there's a human touch to your responses?
And what have you given to your clients recently that will remain on their desk or shelf? Pens, mouse mats and mugs need not apply! Could you make your ideas collectible, too?

Kissing Zone

Virgin trains received a lot of publicity many years ago for putting up a "no kissing" sign on Warrington Bank Quay platform – a tongue-in-cheek reference to the movie Brief Encounter – designed to decrease congestion in drop-off zones. I saw a similar idea at Tallinn International airport. There are a lot of health and safety, and needlessly-negative signs displayed around buildings, nowadays, but here at Tallinn International they give you a positive spin when you wish to drop off or collect a loved one: 15 full minutes to Kiss & Fly. I particularly liked the picture of the lips, just in case it confused would-be travellers.

Wrist Watch

Outside Barcelona airport you will see this rather creative piece of outdoor advertising, by Breitling Watches. They certainly made great use of the cylindrical shape but there was just one thing I would have done... I would have turned the watch around 45 degrees and used the tower structure as a great template for an image of an arm and a wrist. Then, if you wanted to see the brand of the watch, you would need to twist your head – a slight inconvenience, but sure to make you remember the moment and the brand that turned your head.

Black Box Blue Box

I came across an interesting use of advertising space, on my most memorable flight from Zimbabwe to South Africa (as featured in Celebrity Service); the space was inside the on-board box of food with AirLink/ South African Airlines flights. If you were to ever advertise here, what would you do?

Please don't say you'd add a list of services, pictures and testimonials! Think differently, and always think engagement. Perhaps use a quiz with questions to ask your fellow passengers? Answers could be tweeted to your company with the chance of daily prizes!

Budget Cuts?

Not necessarily anything to do with an airport, but certainly worthy of head-turning attention – meet Ryan Hair, a hair salon in London. Quirky business names will always demand a second look.

UP
CLOSE
AND

Personal, of course! The one sure-fire way to grab someone's attention is to make them feel special by personalising all your communications with them, and this will no doubt help you to be remembered.

BUT, and it's a big BUT, personalisation comes at a cost. It takes thought, consideration, and time, but if you have the ability to invest a little of these three attributes you are sure to stand out from the rest.

What's Your Name Sir?

Was it really a coffee chain that created a wave of global publicity by writing your name on the side of your cup? When the announcement was made that your coffee cup would be personalised every time you placed an order, the world went crazy for Starbucks – everyone seemed drawn into the caffeine-laced spell of personalisation as they were made to feel that 'little extra' special. This personalisation gesture has been widely-replicated, but it all started with the global coffee giant.

Remember the Date

Whilst in Manchester with colleagues we visited several potential venues for an upcoming conference. Some were better suited to our needs than others, and two were eventually chosen to host our three-day event.

All of the venues took our contact details, so I was interested to know how they would keep in touch. Only one venue decided we were worth keeping in contact with, but they certainly did it well. It wasn't an e-shot every month, and it wasn't a Christmas brochure; instead, The Point at Lancashire County Cricket Club sent a desk calendar for the coming year, but as you flicked through the pages you began to notice something special...

Chicken Or Tomato?

Growing up in England during the 1970s and '80s presented every poorly child, absent from school, the right to choose one of two food options to make them feel a little better... Heinz chicken or Heinz tomato soup!

Alongside Lucozade and Ribena, these were the staple go-to foods for the unfortunate measles, tonsillitis, chicken pox or flu-stricken child.

Fast forward 30 years, and Heinz embraced the fact their product is synonymous with a quick recovery, leading them to create a wonderful personalised marketing campaign, which I first came across on Facebook.

If you know of a friend, work colleague, or family member who is feeling unwell, you can now buy them a tin of soup and send it to them directly, but this is no ordinary tin of soup: with just a few clicks, you can personalise your recipient's comforting tin of soup with their name!

As soon as I saw the campaign, it stirred memories from my childhood, and I promptly sent a personalised tin to none other than myself...

A few days later the tin arrived with my name in prime position on the side – even in my healthy state, it put a smile on my face, and I know if I had received it as a gift while feeling unwell, it would really have brightened my day.
Best of all, and further-increasing the feel-good factor of Heinz soup, the tin

came with a slip of paper saying that profits from the soup went towards the Starlight Children's Foundation, and the money raised helped to fund pantomime performances of Dick Whittington in children's hospitals at Christmas, for those not fortunate enough to be at home.

What can you personalise in your business? Could you link with a charity or local cause to bring a great feel-good factor to your brand?

Something Different in the Bagging Area

I am fortunate enough to do what I love to do: speak and travel. I am also fortunate to work alongside some amazing speaker agencies and bureaus who represent me worldwide.

When I launched my second book, 'Celebrity Service', I wanted to send the very first copies to all of the bureaus, but I also wanted to send the book with something that was personalised just for them.

Now the obvious way of doing this would be to sign them - but every other speaker does this. No, I wanted to take it a little further, to make the recipients feel extra special.

I designed and created personalised bags. There were two types of bag, a Male and a Female. For all of the female agencies and bookers there was the Diaz, Jolie and (their surname) bag; for the male bag there was Depp, Pitt and (their surname).

It was personalised and quirky, and, of course, it took a little longer to create, but even so, I hadn't expected the response I received via emails and posts on social media... Within moments of them arriving, the following image was posted on Twitter and Facebook:
People still talk about the bags, and some pinned them to the walls in their offices!

 Geoff Ramm retweeted
Gordon Poole Agency @GordonPooleLtd · Jan 29
JP with @GeoffRamm today. Presented with Geoff's new book 'Celebrity Service' in a very unique bag!
#CelebrityService

Personally Speaking

How about this for an OMG Moment? The BE Group hosted the MADE Festival conference for 2,000 entrepreneurs – and they created a Lego figure for every speaker, including a mini Ramm!

OMG Question:

What does personalisation mean to you and your packaging? What could it mean for your customers, clients or associates? So few people take the time, so be the one that does make the effort, and you will become the one that is remembered.

ONE TWENTY

...is all it will take for you and your team to create some truly memorable OMG Moments.

I am often asked how to come up with different, engaging, fun, quirky, and downright crazy ideas, to help businesses stand out from the competition. The answer is a simple one: set yourself no longer than two minutes!

Whether you are with a colleague, a small group, a department, or the entire company, the rules of this system are as follows:

1. Arrange everyone into small groups / teams.

2. Each group receives 1 large sheet of paper and 1 large marker pen.

3. Give everyone the question you need help with. For example: What should we put on our exhibition stand? What offers can we include on the e-shot? How can we tell the world about our new service?

4. Now inform everyone that they only have 2 minutes to come up with as many weird and wonderful, crazy and wacky ideas as possible.

5. Set the clock...

6. Countdown the clock; 1 minute to go, 30 seconds to go, 10 seconds to go, 5,4,3,2,1... that's it; stop what you are writing.

7. Now ask one member from the group to share their ideas with the room.

8. Record the answers.

9. Observe very closely to see what happens in the group... Watch for people's reactions to the ideas, because two things will happen:

> A. Should the group nod politely and say "Yeah that could work", chances are it may work, but it certainly won't be an OMG moment.
>
> B. Should the group burst out laughing, raise their eyebrows, or shout "Oh, you can't do that", chances are you are onto something.

So now you have a shortlist of ideas you never would have dreamt of a few minutes ago.

10 . Now go and develop and then execute those ideas.

Time after time, company after company, and country after country, whenever I have delivered these One Twenty challenges the best and most creative answers are always found within the room.

Plus, having researched the two minute rule since 2002, the results tell me that the most creative answers happen within the first 60 seconds; the next 30 seconds are needed to finalise the idea, and the remaining 30 seconds are used to write up and decide who is going to speak.

You are now just 120 seconds away from some amazing ideas you'd never have thought possible.

The clock is ticking....

Meat the future...

I had the honour of working with the largest FMCG Company in South Africa: Tiger Brands. I spoke at their annual conference in Sun City, and a week later I was invited back, but this time it was to present to everyone in their Marketing departments.

One month later, I returned and met an eighty-strong team of marketeers. I delivered a similar keynote talk to the one in Sun City, but as this was a half-day event I was able to include the One Twenty Challenge to bring the teams together and to test the creativity of the group, encouraging them to generate ideas they had never thought of before.

Months later I received a few messages from colleagues of the Tiger Brands team. From that half day session, Natalie Roberts, who headed up the packaged meats division had come up with an outstanding idea. One of the products she was marketing was polony – a large meat sausage. Now if you've ever purchased large packed meats there is a

slight problem (unless you are a big eater): once you open, cut, store, eat, store, eat, it will start to dry out after a couple of days, and therefore wastage can occur. After the session, Natalie came up with a concept that could actually solve this ongoing problem. She spoke to research and development and, created a prototype of the Enterprise Polony Cap: a yellow plastic cap which attached itself to the end of the product, that not only acts as an air tight seal, but also a guide to cut straight slices. The product was backed by a television commercial which you can find on YouTube by searching Enterprise Polony.

The Result: It was trialled across supermarkets in Southern Africa and sales soared to a 53% increase.

Two minutes. Just Two Minutes. It Works. Try It. Do It. And tell me your successes.

Tata Treasure

Having spent a day presenting to the entire TATA Communications team in Mumbai I received this amazing and unexpected notification on Facebook. 18 months on from our event, the team created two OMG ideas which went on to win two DMA Asia ECHO awards 2015.

SIZE STILL MATTERS

In my first OMG book, I discussed the need to break out of the mould, away from the standard shape and size marketing materials: the A5 flyer, and the tri-fold brochure – templates that blight our creativity and are sure to blend in, rather than stand out.

For years, now, I've been on a global quest to rid the world of such conformity and blandness, whether it's in the freezing depths of Winnipeg or beside the Rocky Steps in Philadelphia, this really is a worldwide epidemic.

As I've travelled far and wide, the strangest thing has started to happen: clients, audience members, friends and associates have also taken up the quest, spotting culprits around the globe, and taking photographs to send to me as evidence…

"Looks Geoff here's another one!!!"

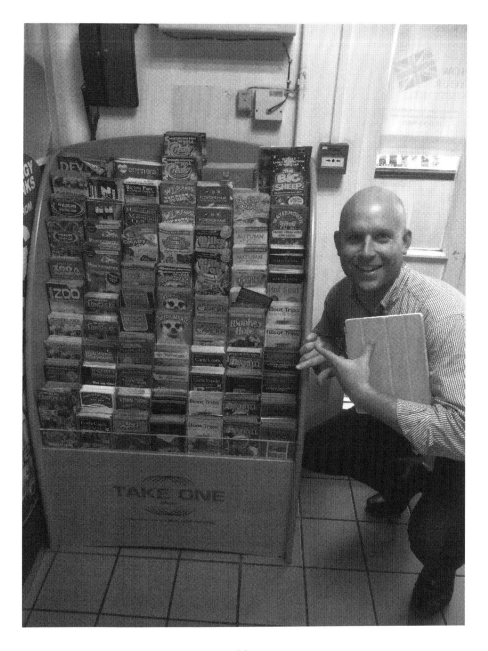

So brochures, flyers, cards, and paper are all dead?

NO... Wait until you read the next few pages.

White Van Woman

One of the greatest examples I've ever seen of using promotional materials to truly target a market, came from Karen Griffin, of Griffin Designs, based in West Sussex, England. They specialise in vehicle livery, and have two clear target customer groups – businesses with poor signage, and others with no signs at all.

Whenever Karen saw a vehicle with zero or poor signage, she'd place a piece of card on their windscreen… But this was no ordinary flyer drop, irritating your poor windscreen wipers - this was an OMG moment.

The card folded up into a model of a white van, but across the sides and doors were the message and contact details of Karen's design company.

Karen told me: "In a nutshell, I was struggling to contact my target market for the mobile signwriting side of the business which is a key summer income stream. I spent a fortune on Google AdWords and they weren't working." A long, cold spring had all but dried up the word of mouth that this service relied on.

"A few calls to past customers, asking them a series of ever refined questions, made me realise that my target market (tradesmen based within a 25 mile radius of Chichester) did not spend a lot of time on the internet, and in fact not many of them even had websites, fewer had smart phones. (Duh! that was why AdWords were not working then!) Yet everywhere we went, there were plain clothes vans parked up around small development sites.

"The first 10 promotional cards (left under windscreen wipers) yielded 8 jobs. The next ten yielded 6 customers to sign-write. Not only was the response rate fantastic, targeted, local (actually it is running at just over 50% at the moment) but we are now back to pinging from job to job as we tend to attract an audience as we work and hand out business cards to them, which results in organic enquiries.

"Furthermore, like AdWords, if we are too busy (feast or famine is the main challenge here) we can easily switch the enquiries off by stopping handing them out! It has been our best marketing idea yet, and is costing us less than £3 per actual customer."

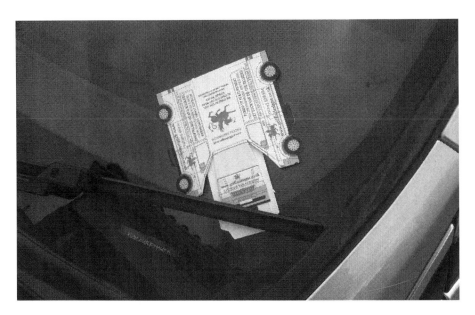

3D 33

Scottish Cup Final Day, Celtic versus Hibernian, Glasgow versus Edinburgh, and a packed national stadium where the terraces were as green as the pitch.

As an Englishman devoted to the red and white stripes, I'll admit it was not the obvious place to be on a summer's afternoon. I was there with five friends: Paul McGee, Andy Lopata, Jeremy Nicholas, Alan Stevens and Stu Harris, and we all shared four things in common: speaking, a love for football, we were good friends of Kenny Harris – a fine speaker on creativity, who sadly died a year before; and we were also there to support number 33 for Hibernian, Kenny's son Alex.

The day was a wonderful and emotional occasion, and despite the final result it was a very proud day for the Harris family. So what has this got to do with marketing?

On the way to Hampden Park stadium, I came across the programme stall which featured a notice: 'Cup Final Programmes – Special Edition'. So apart from being the final, what was so special about this programme? The programme was apparently the world's first 3D programme, complete with cardboard glasses, so the players, interviews, and sponsors came to life on every page.

Thought: Despite 3D glasses being an older invention, they have made a resurgence in recent years in cinemas across the world, so could you use an idea like this to literally 'stand out' from the crowd?

I think Kenny would have loved this piece of OMG creativity.

Love Fool

February the 14th, the most romantic day in the calendar.

Hayley and I have never really done the whole overpriced chocolates, flowers and three-course meal thing; instead we buy a card, we write the card, we swap the cards, and in the morning it appears on the mantelpiece for a week before being shredded and recycled a week later – not the most romantic reading you'll do today, but there you have it.

So picture the scene, February 14th 11:35am, both cards are beside each other on the mantelpiece. I am working on a brand new video with my creative ace Ian West, and in walks Hayley, passing me my post (a magazine I subscribe to and a hand-written letter on top). Thinking nothing of it, I put them to the side, as Hayley walked out of the room. After a few minutes I decided to open the letter- it was, after all, hand-written.

As I turned it over, I froze! You see, we don't play jokes on each other, so I thought "uh oh, what on earth is this?"
So I quickly placed it back, unopened, and slid it under the magazine.

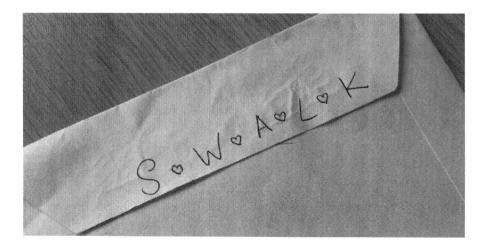

12 hours had passed; Hayley was asleep and I snuck off into the next room. I opened the card/letter

I opened it
Now there's a web link with my name on it... It must be a video message or a picture or two????

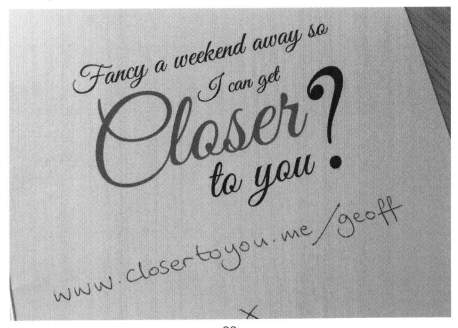

Would you go to the link?   Of course you would! But what was it? And who, for that matter, was it from?!

Nervously, I turned the PC on, and then stretched to place my foot by the door and clicked the link...

OMG!

There was a landing page with a competition. Phew!!!

Hello ...

Thanks for 'getting closer to me'. That romantic night away could still be on the cards! All you now need to do is read the text below and answer a simple question

Good luck and hopefully we can catch up soon.

In the latest radio industry Rajar results Metro Radio and Magic 1152 are pleased to report another impressive set of audience figures! Combined, the stations reach 529,000 people across the region every week.

Metro, as a Sony Award winning station in 2013, has seen sustained growth across 2013 and now has 450,000 weekly listeners. This is the highest figure for 8 years and 177,000 more than its nearest commercial competitor Capital who have 286,000 listeners.

Metro recorded its highest breakfast show figures for 10 years. The market leading Steve and Karen Breakfast Show has seen significant growth with weekly listeners increasing from 251,000 to 281,000 giving them the number one position in the mornings.

Sister station Magic continues to perform well with 147,000 weekly listeners tuning in on

It was a competition from the Bauer Media group.

OMG part two – As you could imagine I was delighted, but not for the reason you might think. You see, this is my client. In my final event of the year, just days before Christmas, I delivered a keynote talk and an OMG interactive workshop to the entire radio teams of Bauer, and challenged them to create moments that will be remembered in over 30 years time. In just two months they did exactly that, and they turned the idea on me! I rang Dominic Munnelly, the Sales Director, the next day and he told me they sent out 200 Valentines cards to commercial businesses, and over 70% responded via the competition. The responses lead to engagement, which lead to meetings, which have since lead to generating clients and creating radio campaigns.

Type 'Great B2B marketing' into Google and it almost becomes a Googlewhack - there is not much there at all, but for me, this was the finest I've seen.   It is amazing what you can come up with using the OMG One Twenty Challenge.

That's right, **THIS IDEA CAME FROM THE TWO MINUTE CHALLENGE!**

OMG CHALLENGE:

You are launching an organic café in the heart of a small village. All of your produce is of the highest quality, and all of it is locally sourced. Your brand is authentic in every way. Everything about you typifies your dedication to recycling, organic products, and the environment.   The seats inside are old pews from church vestibules; the light shades are recycled kitchen colanders... you get the picture.

Now, you have to let the general public know you are open for business.

You want to use flyers to give out to people on the street and push through the letterboxes, but of course this would mean you would have to use paper – and recycled paper is not allowed. How would you do it?

OMG MOMENT:

Luisa Minchella is the entrepreneur of Happy Organic in Cleadon Village. It's a wonderful café and store, which, like all businesses, needed to attract customers through the door. I was set with the challenge of putting something in a potential customers hands – but could not use paper. Later in that very first meeting, I had an idea...

Using the flyers and leaflets which came through our doors, we decided to do some recycling – not by putting them in the bin, but by turning the flyers/leaflets over, then using natural inks from vegetables that were about to be thrown away, to print the details of the new Happy Organic café. Possibly the greatest example of using a flyer without cutting down any more trees!

SORRY WE ARE ENGAGED

The main aim when creating an OMG moment is to engage a person enough to make them slow down, stop, connect, record the OMG, then act on and share it.

Here are some of the best examples I've found, that have stopped me in my tracks and stood out from the competition.

Winnipeg Cars

How can we encourage children to eat more fruit and vegetables? A question I imagine almost every government in the western world wants the answer to. Well, maybe the answer lies in an indoor market in the city of Winnipeg, Canada, or "Winterpeg", as it's locally known.

There were dozens of stalls and stores at The Forks venue, but one business selling fresh fruit and vegetables decided they'd attract attention using a rather well known Disney theme. For half an hour, I watched many parents taking photos of their children beside the Disney-themed stall, and the children picking the produce whilst their parents paid.

Is this the answer to excite children into eating healthier, nutritious food? National governments, please take note.

Melbourne Mocha

Coffee shops and cafes have become the hotbeds of the creative chalkboard era, and this one from Dukes in downtown Melbourne used humour to capture readers attention.

Malta Magic

Two quotes, that's all it took to slow me to a standstill. Either side of the RVS shoe, bags and accessories shop, beneath the windows, were two great and relevant quotes. I took the photographs and then shared via social media, which was another big hit of social engagement. For readers of my first two books, you will no-doubt remember Alison from the world-famous BP petrol station in Johannesburg, and she decided to feature the quotes on her blackboard, too.

Take a further walk into Valetta, and along the wonderful cobbled streets you will see many boutique stores, but this art shop caught my attention - we've all seen these before, the cut-outs which you put your head inside so that a friend, family member or passer-by can take a pic for you. They're the sort of shot that's an instant hit on social media, so you share away, and the associated brand gets an extra hit of exposure – that's why companies love them so much!

Menorca Bear

As if you needed any further proof of the 'cut out' example, here we have it: our daughter, Grace, peeping through the Natura bear in Menorca. These ideas serve as a magnet for passers-by and shouldn't be overlooked if you've got space to play with.

Russell Payne & Co.

What do you think a firm of accountants could put on a sign in their car park?

You have an image in your mind right now, don't you? Possibly an image of negativity in a strict business-to-business style of communication: Clients Only! We Can Not Take Responsibility For Your Vehicle or its Belongings! Etc., etc., etc.

Well, not with my client, Russell Payne and Co. Russell is a great character, and he likes to do things a little differently; he simply loves to engage... Check out this sign and I wonder how many times you'll smile as you read every bullet point?

You don't have to have a high street presence to perform such engagement; how about in the reception of your office, or on your next exhibition stand?

PICK AND MIX

A selection of pictures taken throughout my observational travels.

A. BBQ Marinades point of sale as a Barbeque

B. Johnsons Baby products as creatively seen in a pram / travel system

C. Ringtons Tea delivery van seeing the opportunity with the name of the vehicle

D. A great head turner by the vehicle promoting the model village in Babbacombe, Torquay

E. Bar & Shoes, Menorca, one side of the shop sold shoes, the other served wine – could this be the perfect fusion marketing business idea?

F. Fantastic word play and branding taken from the famous Only Fools and Horses hit tv show.

G. Wonderful quirky messaging from the Citizen M hotel chain

H. Another great head turner from Noah's Ark Zoo Farm – but this time they are encouraging you to spot the elephant, take a photograph, and tag them on Facebook for the chance to win tickets into the Zoo!

I. Super idea from iconic UK fashion brand Superdry – outside their store they've placed deckchairs and a further selfie competition via Twitter, Facebook and Instagram to win vouchers!

101

GOD MEET THE DINOSAURS

Holy Inappropriate?

The Duomo di Milano has to be the most photographed and visited attraction in Milan. Every inch of its stunning architecture is begging to be photographed against the crystal blue skies above. But when renovations to the stonework are underway, there is a very opportunistic business side to religion that kicks in.

On the sides of the building where the work is taking place, there are a number of advertising spaces for sale. There will be many who dislike this approach, and I have to admit, it had me thinking whether it was appropriate behaviour by the church, or just a clever way to raise funds by offering to promote brands to every passer-by. I noticed there were many brands that took up the offer of this prime advertising display space, including Longchamp and Mercedes.

Malta Merc

To coincide with the release of the Summer blockbuster, Jurassic World, Mercedes were prominent, once again. As the main vehicle sponsor of the movie, they can be easily seen on the silver screen, but, similar to placing cars at the Metro Centre a week before Christmas, they also thought of using their product in a shopping mall. In Silema, Malta, they set the scene with a miniature version of Jurassic World, complete with electrified fences and warning signs. As you walked through the set you could have your photo taken with a model dinosaur, with the car in the background, of course.

Tee Rex

Whilst I am on the subject of our extinct friends... I met the entrepreneur behind a mini golf business, located in Tynemouth, on the North East coast of England. His course is next to a main road, behind a raised embankment. Business was okay, but unless you were sat on the upstairs of a double decker bus, you couldn't see that the golf course was there. To raise his profile and turn some heads, he turned the course into a Dinosaur themed area, adding giant dinosaurs whose heads now leer over the embankment and are clearly visible to passers-by. Almost overnight the investment in the dinosaurs caused footfall and turnover to double.

Erring on the side of patriotism, I would have hoped the Duomo di Milano would use their advertising space to promote Italian brands, or to boost small, local businesses, or even a charity.

Mercedes could have taken their dinosaur theme further, perhaps with a T-Rex-sized chunk taken out of the door, or allowing visitors to Jurassic world to sit inside the safety of the vehicle as the dinosaurs attacked around them. For me that would have made for a much greater action shot which may have just tempted me to walk through Jurassic World and share my experience on social media.

STAND AND DELIVER

Exhibitions, expos, networking events, you've probably been to them all, and maybe you've even taken a stand yourself, to promote your business.

Once you have purchased your space, you now produce a marketing checklist of the things you need to make this space a success for you...

Here is what many of those checklists look like:

1. Pull up banner stands (with lights on top, if you are flush!)
2. A5 leaflets and/or trifold brochures
3. Giveaways (mouse mats, pens, usb sticks etc.)
4. The 'Child Catcher from Chitty Chitty Bang Bang' bowl of sweets
5. Table and chair
6. Laptop (normally showing your website or corporate video)
So where is the engagement? Where is the excitement? Where is your

competitive edge from every other stand owner? They may not be your direct competitors, but for the duration of this event they most certainly are – competing for attendee time and interaction.

Without careful thought and planning, it's easy to become just another forgotten face in the exhibiting crowd.

Here are my top tips for making your stand a stand-out:

Think excitement, think competition and think noise – you want to hit the senses of visitors nearby, to make them wonder what is going on. Most of all: think fun!

Just because the delegates may be business people, they're not immune to having some fun, and, for a few minutes, being a child again! You also want your team manning the stand to enjoy the day - it may just keep them off their mobile phones, and from hiding behind the table nibbling on a sandwich!

1. Leaflets and brochures – think ARGOS Catalogue. If you must have leaflets or brochures, stack them high in one pile; don't think you need to fan them out to make a pretty pattern. People will not want to disturb your pretty pattern and therefore won't take your materials!

2. DO NOT SIT BEHIND YOUR TABLE. The table acts as a barrier between you and the attendee, making you seem less approachable, and making interactions feel less natural. If you need a table or chair, put it to the side of your stand and try to move away from it as much as possible.

3. Laptops showing corporate videos – NO! You are the best thing an attendee can watch and speak with. There's no reason to display you website, either – the people manning your stand should be letting attendees know who you are and what you do, not your home page.

4. Look to stimulate as many senses as possible – can people see something exciting? Can they hear something different? Can they taste your product when they are there? Can they touch, play with or smell things on your stand?

To help you further I have highlighted some of the very best stands I've ever seen – I hope they inspire you...

Hello Creativity

Say bonjour to Simon Jones, of Bonjour Photography. He's a photographer specialising in schools photography. I came across him at an event for Boarding Schools; there were a dozen or so stands around the main area, and only a couple stood out.

Observing Simon's stand, I watched the delegates walk away with a gift box in their hands and smiles on their faces.

Intrigued, I went over to speak to him and asked what he was giving away. His response was an OMG moment!

In the build up to the conference, the exhibitors received a list of the schools who were attending. Question: What would you do with this list?

Simon sent out an email to everyone who was attending, saying how he was looking forward to meeting them, then he asked a simple question 'What is your favourite chocolate?' He then promised that when they replied to the question their chocolate of choice would be waiting for them at his stand on the day of the event!!!

Weeks later, a stream of delegates queued up at his stand to engage with Simon and receive their chocolate. He went one step further, though, and also gave each delegate an additional gift box which included a mini bottle of wine.

I asked Simon what the response rate was to his email, he told me over 90%, which meant a heavy footfall of attendees heading direct to his stand, interacting with him, and walking away with a strong, positive, memorable impression of Simon and his business.

Fruity Bear

The other exhibition stand that stood out that day was from a marketing and branding agency, The Barley House Group, and their stand was a fruit stall.

One of their main services is designing exhibition stands for schools, so they demonstrated their own skills to deliver their message brilliantly.

To prove this was no one-off idea, I met them again that same year whilst speaking at another schools event. This time they created a coconut shy style fairground attraction, where attendees used an air gun to knock down as many tin cans as they could. Everyone, and I mean everyone, received a gift for taking part – a rather cute Barley Bear cuddly soft toy with the brand on its t-shirt.

So this stand had something exciting on it, a gift for taking part; but best of all.... it had an interactive social media twist. Beside the fairground attraction was a giant 6ft Cuddly Bear which you could also win, but not for knocking down the tin cans. Around the neck of the small bear was a tag, so all you needed to do was take a photo of the bear in a creative place and share it on Twitter via the hashtag. The most creative photograph won the Giant Bear.

The Sum Of All Jumps

At the Chartered Institute of Management Accountants event, there was only one exhibition space that caused a swarm of delegates.

Grant-Jones Accountancy installed a games console with a winter Olympic ski jump game. The rules were simple – jump the furthest and you would win a Galaxy Tab2 prize. A leader board was introduced so people could see what they had to do to win, and to check that they had not been overtaken – a great way to ensure people keep coming back!

The Stars In A Reasonably Priced Car

Zoe Easey and Will King from Epix Media, Lincolnshire, exhibited at the Marketing Expo alongside 50 other companies, but they were the ones with the OMG idea.

They used the exhibition table as a test track for a remote controlled car. They added challenges to the course which meant you had to drive the remote controlled car through various obstacles which they had nicknamed 'Twitter feed' lane, 'Google Chrome' roundabout, etc., all designed to test your driving skills as you navigated your way back into the 'Ebay' stop. The fastest time won a box of chocolates.

Just Quackers

Managing Director, Marcia Gomez, and her team at the luxury serviced apartments, Cotels, were looking to attract attention to their stand at the BT Show in Olympia, London. She told me the previous year that they had very little impact, attracting 5 contacts at the most. But this year was different; this year they increased their contacts by over 600%.

Here is how they did it…

A large cardboard cut-out of a twitter screen dangled down in front of the stand for people to stick their heads through, take a picture and tweet

it to their followers, while the whole stand was sprinkled by the brand's signature plastic ducks, which are seen in all their luxury apartments. The ducks and the interactive cut-out brought a lot of footfall to their stand throughout the day, and increased their traction by spreading on social media.

Marcia added 'The ideas on the stand were fun and different to what we had previously displayed so it certainly motivated the team, which I believe helped us achieve greater success.'

Nash Bridges

Moving away from the more corporate style of exhibiting, I want to show you a piece of marketing brilliance that had me laughing all the way along the Quayside in Newcastle upon Tyne.

On a Sunday morning, market traders descend onto the quayside from the Tyne Bridge along to the Millennium Bridge, where you will find David Nash. He sells all kinds of wallets, purses, bags and other leather items, but it's his sense of humour and his amazing OMG signs that have you stopping to read them all...

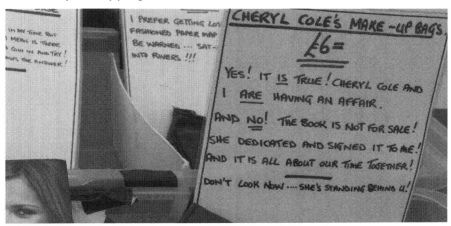

Face Lift

This has nothing to do with Stand And Deliver, however, it is a very different take on using the materials of a pull up banner stand to capture the eye in a shopping mall.   The mall in question was Manor Walks in Cape Town and this was also the scene of the very first OMG video.

Whilst walking around the complex, I noticed on the other side from me was a lift, but when customers pressed the button and it began to rise... that's when Nivea decided to give their marketing a face lift.

Busy Buzzy

I was honoured to be the opening keynote speaker at the ISMM conference at the Ricoh Arena. I was all set for the event when the client said I could also have a stand in the exhibition area. I would be alongside hundreds of marketing and sales companies who, let's face it, know a thing or two about exhibiting and standing out.

It was time for a host of OMG thoughts and ideas to come together in one space. This is what I did:

1. Maximised the space by producing posters rather than take pull up banner stands.
2. Stacked my books (Argos catalogue style) so people could pick one up.
3. Displayed a large 'buzzer' machine – you know the one where you navigate a metal hook around the machine – trying not to touch the sides and make it BUZZ!!!
4. Created a competition – the winner with the fastest time around the buzzer machine, without touching the sides, won a box of Milk Tray – the brand that started my obsession with marketing.

The result? Queues formed around my stand, all day. My colleague and I spoke to many delegates and discussed several possible future events (two further bookings came as a result). I also signed and sold copies of my books. However, the 'buzzer' game was the tipping point – it was the magnet that attracted people, as they could see and hear it from across the room.

Bonus result! Take a closer look at the image. The photographer featured our stand in a write-up in a local newspaper a week later.

OMG Questions To Consider:

How will you Stand And Deliver?

What are you going to give away?

What game could you play?

What could be the incentive to entice delegates to visit you?

How many senses can you target to gain attention?

TWO SCOOPS

Feeling creative? Feeling lucky? Feeling like another OMG One-Twenty Challenge?

Here you go…

You own an ice cream parlour. You have over 50 flavours of home-made ice cream on offer, as well as wonderful home-made fudge, sweets and candies. To attract passing trade, you've placed numerous signs and billboards outside, as well as the essential giant ice cream cone.

There is, however, one problem:

Your next door neighbour, the business right next door, is selling exactly the same products, and they are promoting themselves in exactly the same way! In fact, your ice cream competitor also has a garden and patio area at the back so customers can sit down and relax with their purchases!

So the golden question is - how are you going to differentiate yourself to entice customers into your parlour?
You know what happens next, set your clock to two minutes, press start, and write down all the marketing ideas that pop into your head.

GO!

Your 5 OMG Ideas:

1. _____

2. _____

3. _____

4. _____

5. _____

Times up. Did you succeed? Did you create ideas you could develop to help you stand out?

All of the challenges and observations featured in my books are real examples, and this tasty example was observed on a family holiday in Somerset.

Got it Licked

We spent a fantastic day exploring the caves and sites at Cheddar Gorge. The main street was full of gift shops and eateries, and towards the bottom of the Gorge are two ice cream parlours.

We scratched our heads, wondering why two businesses selling exactly the same thing in the same way would want to set up beside each other (OK, I scratched my head; Hayley, Grace and Elliot were focused on the ice creams we were about to eat). We walked across the road to see which flavours we would choose.

Outside the shop on the left was a young gentleman, holding a tray of fudge samples. Everyone who walked past was asked the following question: "Would you like to try some of our handmade fudge?"

Everybody, and I mean everybody (including us), said yes; they stopped, and as they chose a piece of fudge he told them about some of the flavours of ice cream they made and sold in-store. We walked, in bought three ice creams and a bar of the fudge we'd just sampled.

Five days later, we returned to Cheddar Gorge.

Guess which shop we went back to?

It may not be the most qualitative or indeed quantitative piece of research you'll ever encounter in your life, but for these two visits, the parlour with the fudge samples was full on both occasions.

Coincidence or differentiation? I'll let you decide.

WHAT
COMPETITION?

Competition is a good thing, yes? It should keep you on your marketing toes, and help to propel your service levels to Celebrity standards.

But how do you make yourself stand out from and above your competitors? What are your competitive advantages? What makes people choose you, and keep coming back?

The following observations are a selection of competitive stories which are worthy of consideration next time you look to gain the upper hand…

Licked Clean

Your car needs an all-round good, quick, inexpensive clean. Thankfully you have four car-wash companies within a two mile radius, so which do you choose?

To help you make up your mind, consider the following:

Two of the companies are national recognised brands; two are independent businesses.

The national brands have a wide range of car-cleaning services (8 to be precise) and different prices to choose from; the independents only have 3 options.

The signage and layout of the national brands are far more appealing to the eye than the independents, which have poor brand consistency on their signage, and are set up on disused wastelands.

So who would you choose?

If you are still undecided, let me help you by asking a 3 year old little boy called Elliot Ramm. As he's sat in the back of the car, I say: "C'mon Elliot let's go to get Daddy's car washed." His response? "Lollipops, lollipops, lollipops…"

We drive a couple of miles to one of the independent car washes. We pull up, hand brake on, then the car is soaked, sprayed, foamed, and hand-dried. Then, right at the end, at the point of passing over the money, the back door opens and one of the team reach over to Elliot with a box of lollipops for him to choose from.

And there is the OMG moment, and the real reason why this business gets our business, every time.

Come Back Later

This is a great sales technique which encourages you to come back to Starbucks rather than go anywhere else: when you buy your coffee in the morning you receive a Treat Receipt which allows you to buy a drink for a reduced price of £2, but only after 2pm, that same day.

What could you introduce to encourage people to choose you and not a competitor next time?

Caffeine Competitors

When we hear or read the word competitor, almost straight away we conjure up thoughts of negativity, yet this next example was both fun and friendly competition from two nearby rivals.

The Lakes Bakery, run by Elliott Johnson in Barrow, is a wonderful bakery which specialises in amazing cake designs. They also sell coffee. As do Costa Coffee, just yards up the same road. One morning Elliott placed this sign outside his shop...

Cue: arguments in the street, a rival board being placed outside, or law enforcement intervention? No.

There was none of that. Instead there was just a flurry of light-hearted messages between the owners of The Lakes Bakery and Costa, exchanged throughout the business day on Twitter and Facebook. Their status comments and general feel-good banter caused a comedy stir in the local area, which helped both businesses to be seen as human.

There have been many cases of brand rivals engaging in this sort of healthy rivalry and banter, with positive results for all involved: search on the internet for 'Audi v BMW checkmate billboard' and 'Pepsi v Coke Halloween', as these are great creative ways in which both brands were highlighted and promoted.

Latte SoftTop

Waiting to meet my clients in the wonderful Fahle Coffee Shop & Restaurant in Tallinn, I noticed that each table had a promotional card offering deals and information about the local Peugeot dealership. I am unsure of the exact relationship between the two companies, however, that question can wait for another time. What I liked most was the collaborative nature of these two businesses coming together to help and promote one another. I would like to think there was something similar in the dealership to promote the coffee shop & restaurant. The cards also featured a QR code to scan so you could instantly have all the dealership details on your phone, for easy reference.

So who is promoting you in your town or village? What offer can you create to encourage a second visit? Or maybe offer a small gift or token to differentiate you from the rest...

CHASE THE ACE
PART DEUX

Are you continuing to put the power of your brand in someone else's hand?

Yes, I am talking about the wonderfully understated and often underused business card.

The shape, the texture, the size, and most of all, the relevance of your card to your business brand, all play significant roles in creating a memorable first and everlasting impression.
Here are a few I've held onto dearly on my travels, so far...

Becki Saltzman - a fellow speaker who talks about 'arousing the buy curious'. I must admit I was a little shocked when she gave me her card at a conference, but it is truly an OMG moment.

Another fellow speaker, Jay Baer, also has something to keep and most definitely use - his card is rather heavy, great quality, and doubles up as a bottle opener.

Former England international and Manchester United defender, Rio Ferdinand, owns a wonderful restaurant in Manchester, called Rosso. Their card doubles up as a magnifying glass, should anyone need a little extra help to read the fine print on the menus!

UK-based print and design specialist, Mark McIvor, created this wonderful bubblegum style card, which includes foil for added effect.

My colleague, Paula Martilla, who I worked with in Tallinn, Estonia, doesn't carry cards. After our event, people were coming up to both of us, asking for our cards; with none to hand out, Paula instead takes one of your own, turns it over, then stamps her details on the back using her printing stamp!

So what about me? Well, my most recent card was a little different - when people ask for my card I say to them "Hold out your hand...", then "If you are looking for a speaker to really stand out at your event" and I give them the card, it pops out, and then unfolds to show "www.geofframm.com".

As a quick side-observation, I am amazed at how much information is printed on cards nowadays: name, title, business name, list of services, YouTube channel, Twitter, LinkedIn, Facebook, email, mobile, office number, address... I prefer just my web address - thereby steering everyone to the mothership – your website.

THE GREAT OUTDOORS

Brand placement and advertising can easily drift down the same old avenues, following tried and tested – and boring – formats. Adding a twist to your message or promotion style can seriously increase your visibility.

I've said for many years that South Africa seems to have an edge when it comes to adding a different dimension to their marketing activities, as these examples demonstrate.

Billbored?

How many billboards actually get noticed, nowadays? Yes, technology has helped by bringing in scrolling boards and even electronic video screens, but you still need a twist to ensure eyes are focused on your message.

Three of the best I've seen on the roads were in the amazingly creative zone known as South Africa...

Highlights!

To promote the Audi S Model, the German car giant added real lights to the car headlights on their billboards. As the skies darkened, you could see these distinctive lights stand out a mile.

Do Put Baby In The Corner!

How would you display the famous Dirty Dancing show on a billboard? Could you use an unforgettable moment from the movie to break outside of the normal rectangular bounds of conformity? Using the iconic 'lift scene' in the following die cut style ensured their billboard ad really stood out.

Suck Up a Pole

When trying to create an OMG moment, always take the time to look at the environment you are in. Is there a piece of material nearby you could use, or a part of the landscape? KFC effectively used the lampposts on the motorway out of Johannesburg as the straw to promote their new milkshakes.

Tea Junction

Head-turning and bang-on-brand was the use of an old-style British mini, by British tea company, Twinings of London, seen here in a shopping mall in Gauteng. Again, a fine example of advertising with a twist – instead of drifting down the typical sandwich-board-outside-the-tea-shop advertising technique, a Mini car replaced it in a brighter, bolder, bigger way!

Oh Christmas Tree...

Back in the UK luxurious retail brand Fortnum & Mason displayed a ginormous Christmas tree at St Pancras train station, London, complete with brand-coloured ribbons and matching gift boxes underneath. In prime position, and tastefully branded throughout, this simply could not be ignored.

ARE YOU OMG READY?

Or are you still in the dark when it comes to taking advantage of the opportunities around you? Are you really ready to think quickly, act positively and make things happen?

Let's see if you can strike the last match of creativity and take advantage of the following...

Here is your final OMG Challenge:

You own a café in the beautiful Derbyshire Dales countryside, which is a real tourist hotspot. Your café is located right beside the entrance to the public car park.

As visitors drive in and park up, they head towards the Welcome & Pay

Here station, which includes useful information about the area and a pay machine to purchase a parking ticket. The machine does not give change.

Visitors are often seen searching for the correct change, but can you help them? Could you possibly deliver a combined OMG Marketing and Celebrity Service moment?

Here's your chance. You decide to stick a notice on the machine, but what will it say? Pick up your pencil and write a message on this blank piece of paper to help your business stand out from the rest...

You have 2 minutes to come up with an idea.

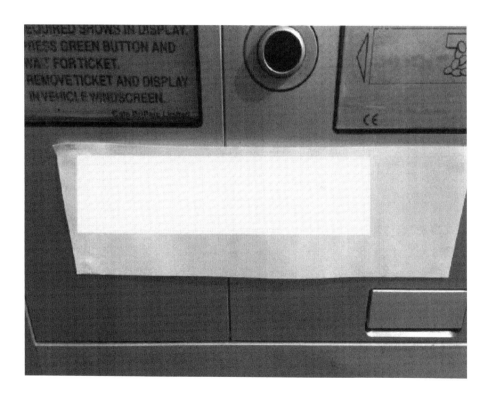

All of my OMG Marketing observations are based on real life examples; now take a look to see for yourself what was written on that parking machine note.

As you can see, not all businesses are ready to see the opportunities.

As my good friend Nigel Risner says, 'Opportunity is nowhere' it's up to you how you interpret this, either as 'now here' or 'no where'.

You have a choice.

SAY
CHEESE

I was sat in my office when, >ping!< the next sales-led email dropped into my inbox.

It was from Pizza Hut.

The subject line was as follows: "Dear Geoff, We Have Revolutionised The Future Of Pizzas".

Ok, now you have my attention. Firstly, it was personalised, and secondly, I really wanted to know how they had revolutionised pizza!

But let us backtrack for a moment, first – how did they obtain my email address and christian name? Well, that was easy: with my first online purchase I received a free garlic bread with cheese – nothing happens without an offer! At the same time, they asked me if I wanted to receive special offers and promotions – like free garlic bread and cheese? Of course I do! Note: they didn't ask "do you want to go on our database?" - a sure-fire way to turn people off. I clicked yes and the following occurred some months later....

Back to my inbox...

Opening the email, I read: 'With our trained chefs we can now create the image of your face using the pizza toppings of your choice, which will then be freshly made and delivered to your home in 45 minutes time...'

It then showed you the following image in the main body of the email I had only one thought... **'NOOOOOOOOOOOOO! O.M.G. How can this be possible?'**

It looked amazing, and yes, they were truly right about the claim to revolutionise the pizza market.

In order to ensure my next pizza had my face on it, I was told I had to do 3 things:

1. Find a head and shoulders photograph as a jpeg image;

2. Copy the image into the box provided, and then press GO;

3. Impatiently wait as the clock counted down from 5 to 0, then the image of your face will be shown on screen before you confirm your order.

Now I'm excited!

So I quickly minimised the screen and searched for some headshots. I found a holiday image and cropped it around my head and shoulders, then re-saved as a jpeg image.

I copied it into the box and pressed GO.

The countdown began.

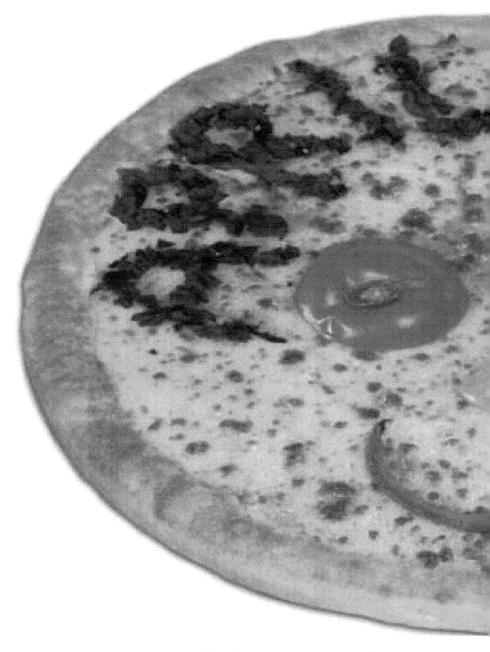

To say I had to pick myself up off the floor would be an understatement. I laughed out loud long before LOL became popular.

I had also forgotten what day it was... 1st April also known as... April Fools Day!

For me it was the finest, most creative email I had ever received, and I have yet to receive any that could match its interaction and engaging style. This email was first received back in April 2009, have you any idea how many people around the world over I have told about Pizza Hut and this OMG email moment?

YOUR
MARKETING
WALL

It's time to take down your motivational posters of mountains and oceans, cats with quotations, and original artwork. You're not going to climb or swim them, and chances are you've not even looked at them in a long while. That "inspirational" wall you had such high hopes for, rapidly becomes just part of the background, and it's time to change that.

The problem with seeing Observational Marketing Greats, is just that - we see them. Then we forget them. We then rarely use them as inspiration for our own future campaigns.

But all this is about to change.

You will, no doubt, have come across some jaw-dropping and head-turning pieces of marketing, whether they are examples of materials, adverts, outdoor, social, or digital marketing wonders, but apart from a momentary giggle, gasp or smile, and maybe a quick share with friends, family and work colleagues, what do you actually do with these ideas?

The answer, probably, is nothing.

Following on from the One Twenty technique, here is my second instalment on how you can continually generate fresh marketing ideas for you and your brand.

Here is what you need to do:

For every email that makes you read, click, and potentially buy from the sender – print it off and stick it on your marketing wall;

For every printed advert that catches your eye then makes you strain your neck to read more, rip it out and stick it on your marketing wall;

For every physical piece of marketing that you open, read ,and react positively to, (you know what to do, don't you?) grab some tape or glue and stick it to your marketing wall;

For every update, app, video, or text message on your smartphone, if it made you act to read more, take a screen grab, print it, and place it on the wall.

You get the picture?

This area in your office, hallway, or canteen, is an OMG Wall that will become full of the marketing stuff you and your team love, and it will act as a great stimulus for creative daily thinking.

It needs to be a visible place for you and your team to see each and every day, to help in the quest to create that OMG moment. These ideas will help reinforce what it was that grabbed your attention and these are the ideas you need to bring to your own activities.

Here is the start of a Marketing Wall which has been set up by Maria Holmes-Keeling, Marketing Manager at Alltruck...

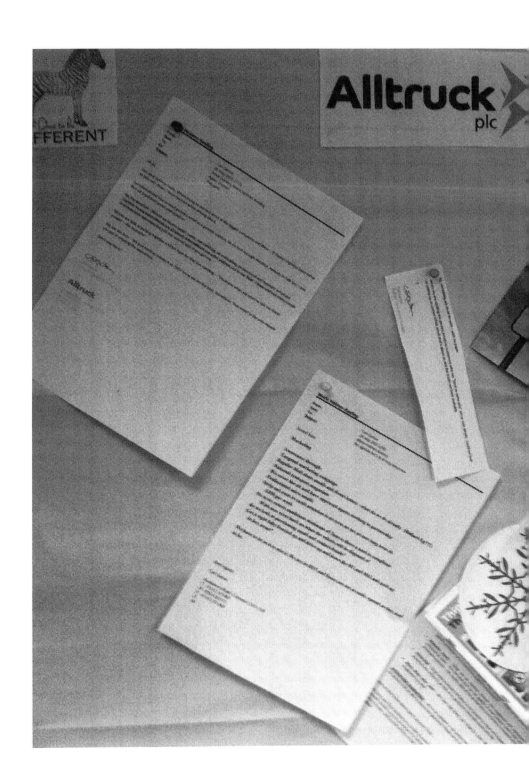

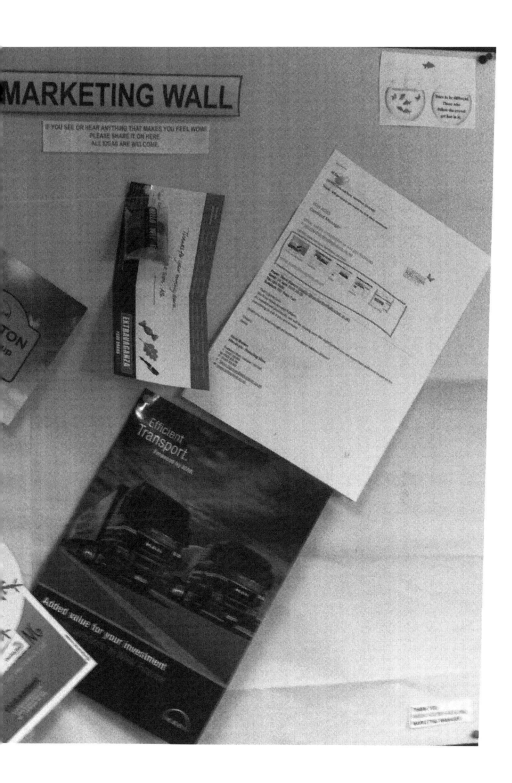

THE END

Well there we have it, the trilogy comes to an end and the circle is complete.

First up there were the original OMG ideas to help you stand out from the crowd, then along came Celebrity Service to ensure you filled the customer service gap, and finally a deluge of Strikes Back ideas to keep your creative juices flowing.

Before I go, an extra special thanks have to go to so many people; the clients, businesses, entrepreneurs and teams around the world who continually seek to surprise and delight, the bureaus and agents who work alongside me, my fellow speakers who I have the honour of sharing a stage with and who continue to inspire me, but most importantly my closet family who support this cider, pizza loving Sunderland supporter on this wonderful journey.

And finally, don't be seduced by the dark side of marketing and customer service, where conformity rules and average excels.

Become a creative rebel, og eht rehto yaw, and become the one everyone is talking about.

Wishing you every future success.

Made in the USA
San Bernardino, CA
16 April 2017